CHURCH, PRAY

How to Walk in Spiritual Authority
through the Power of Prayer

BISHOP ARTHUR F. MOSLEY

Foreword by Bishop Jerry W. Macklin

CHURCH, PRAY

How to Walk in Spiritual Authority
through the Power of Prayer

BISHOP ARTHUR F. MOSLEY

Foreword by Bishop Jerry W. Macklin

MEWE
Lithonia, GA

Scripture references are taken from various versions and translations of the Holy Bible. Pronouns for referring to the Father, Son, and Holy Spirit are capitalized intentionally and the words satan and devil are never capitalized.

Publisher:
MEWE, LLC
www.mewellc.com

First Edition
ISBN: 979-8-9871970-3-5

Library of Congress Control Number: 2023906300

Printed in the United States of America.

To my amazing wife, ministry partner, and best friend, Shelia, who has encouraged me to do my God-given, divine assignment with passion and excellence. You are the love of my life.

TABLE OF CONTENT

ACKNOWLEDGEMENTS

I would like to thank my church family, the Cathedral of Faith Church of God in Christ in Atlanta, Georgia, and my family.

Cathedral has been a wonderful source of inspiration and strength in completing this work. I love and appreciate every member for their prayers, kindness, love, and support.

My family has constantly supported and encouraged me to press forward in my kingdom duties.

Special thanks to Sharon Dunn and Leo Brown for their assistance with editing.

FOREWORD

Bishop Arthur F. Mosley is a dynamic and compassionate expositor of the Word of God. His message is one of hope, that is deeply rooted in scripture and the salvation of Jesus Christ. He has been so richly blessed with the anointing of God that gives him the spiritual benediction necessary to reach people from all walks of life as he introduces them to the life-giving, life-changing Savior.

Church, Pray is a book that exudes the pure essence of Bishop Mosley. In this book, Mosley calls us to three things: focus, conversation with God, and community. He encourages us to focus our time, surroundings, and our being on the Almighty. This focus, Mosley asserts, will bring us a renewed mindset and excitement to the power of prayer.

When calling us to conversation with God, Mosley stresses the importance of not only talking to God but listening to God. Therefore, reinforcing the didactic nature of prayer.

Lastly, we are called to community. Bishop Mosley reinforces the significance of prayer being a key construct of the church, and how together we all benefit from prayer.

I am confident that after reading this book, your vigor will be renewed about the power of prayer. Prayer is essential to the vitality of the church and God's people; we cannot live without it. "For thine is the kingdom, and the power, and the glory, forever. Amen."

Bishop Jerry W. Macklin
Hayward, CA

INTRODUCTION

Many of us face a common crisis in life. We find ourselves exhausted, overcommitted, and just hanging on to our schedules by a thread. This is true of us as believers, and also true of us as the church. We are struggling to connect with both the churched and unchurched; we find it challenging to grow in our relationship with God; and we have a hard time growing our ministries. When we pray, our minds wander off in many directions. We have so many distractions bombarding our thoughts.

What is the root of the problem? We need to refocus. We must hear the voice of God and obey it. Prayer is communication. Remember, effective communication requires attentive listening. To hear God, we have to take time to listen. Just like any other conversation, prayer must be a time to focus not only on talking but on being a good listener. To achieve this, it's critical to take the time to listen during prayer instead of being focused on filling the space with our own words. God has incredible things to say to us, things that will change our very lives and the church forever.

It's time to pray, openly, honestly, and vulnerably, because that kind of prayer leads to revival. We need the Holy Spirit to sweep through our churches like wildfire, igniting the hearts and souls of everyone present. That kind of spark is contagious and will reignite every aspect of not only our lives but our churches and ministries. Other people will catch it and we will multiply disciples, all working in unison for the cause of the Gospel.

It all starts with us, as individuals and as a church, returning to prayer and remembering its power. If you haven't seen the impact of prayer in your life and your church recently, it's not because prayers are not powerful, it's that we aren't utilizing the authority God has granted us. As God's children, we are given the opportunity to wield His power for the cause of furthering His plan and purpose for this world.

Not only that, but through prayer, God brings powerful revelations to our lives. Jeremiah 33:3 (NLT) reads, "Ask me and I will tell you remarkable secrets you do not know about things to come." Notice the Lord's invitation to us; that is, He invites us to ask, request, make an appeal, or call. The Lord is offering us the opportunity to come into His presence, be His guest, and receive His help. He welcomes us to do this in the spirit of reverence and worship. Most importantly, we are assured of His responding positively and powerfully. He promised to answer by speaking and doing. He wants to blow our minds. Through the consistent disciplines of reading God's Word and prayer, God shares His infinite wisdom with us. God not only gives us the ability to carry out His will for our lives, but He directs us toward it.

In this book, we are going to do a deep dive into the power of prayer. We are going to discuss the importance of obedience, walking in spiritual authority through the power of prayer, keeping in tune with God's presence, and refocusing our ears to hear the voice of God in the midst of our loud, cluttered world.

At the end of our time together, I pray that you understand this truth: That prayer is both a simple but remarkably powerful thing. All we need to do to wield the power of God is to seek Him with all our hearts. In Luke 11:9 (NLT), Jesus says, "And so I tell you, keep on asking, and you will receive what you ask for. Keep on seeking, and you will find. Keep on knocking, and the door will be opened to you." Asking, seeking, and knocking are all commands. Hence, we must pray. We must be relentless in our pursuit of God. It's crucial that we continually return to Him, seeking Him out even when life is at its hardest. We must stay spiritually focused, even when it seems as if the entire world around us has been enveloped in worldly pursuits.

Our key to pursuing God is in prayer. Through prayer, He is accessible to us 24/7. It doesn't matter who we are, where we are, or what time it is: God is present when we reach out to Him through prayer. It's time for us to rise up, both as individuals and as the church, and harness the incredible power of prayer.

Bishop Arthur F. Mosley

CHAPTER ONE

Listen and Obey

Sometimes the simplest of instructions are the most ignored and the most challenging. It is as if we hear, but we do not *listen;* we read words on a page, but do not let their meaning register in our heads and hearts. We tend to think this is typical of children, but it happens to adults just as well. These barriers are the things that are pulling our attention away from what we should be listening to and comprehending.

What Are the Barriers?

One glaring example of such barriers is our dislike of the person who is giving the instructions. We have no objection to the content as such, but when we realize who is speaking, we are instantly turned off by their message. And how many of us have the habit of getting our answers ready in our minds while the other person is still talking? While they are still giving out information, we are formulating an argument—in other words, we are not listening.

Another barrier is daydreaming, which is like being in another world at the moment. It is amazing the number of times that there is an outpouring and a great move of God— He is present, and His glory is evident—and then you see some people not even responding and not receiving the spiritual blessing the anointing brings. Why? Because they have something else on their minds – they are distracted. They are worried about their bills, their own physical ailments, their children, their elderly parents, and so on. For others, their emotions could have gotten the better of them, so, they continue to harbor anger, disappointment, or distrust. They are not in the right frame of mind to receive the message.

Another common barrier is when the listener has already made up their mind about what they want to do regardless of the instructions. I have learned, as a pastor, that when folk come into my office and tell me, "The Lord said this or that," they are actually telling me to be quiet and just listen to them. They are lacking a willing heart to be open to my instructions and guidance.

Examples of Hearing but Not Listening

In Scripture, we find countless examples of people who heard but did not listen. Adam and Eve heard but did not listen:

And the LORD God commanded the man, saying, you may surely eat of every tree of the garden but of the tree of the knowledge of good and evil you shall not eat of it, for on the day that you eat of it you shall surely die (Genesis 2:16-17 ESV).

Yes, they heard the instruction not to eat or consume the fruit of this specific tree, but here is the proof they did not listen:

Now the serpent was more crafty than any other beast of the field that the LORD God had made. The serpent said to the woman, "Did God actually say 'You shall not eat of any tree in the garden'?" (Genesis 3:1 ESV)

The devil was not directly disputing God's command. No, he was more subtle than that; he asked an indirect question intending to make Eve doubt what God had explicitly said. In effect, he was insinuating that God could not be trusted at His word — *"Did God actually say…?"* Is this what God is truly calling for?

The woman answered innocently and naïvely, *"We may eat of the fruit of the trees in the garden…"* (Genesis 3:2).

Eve told the serpent that God said, *"You shall not eat of the fruit of the tree that is in the midst of the garden, neither shall you touch it, lest you die"* (Genesis 3:3 ESV). God did not say, "…neither shall you touch it." (See Genesis 2:16-17).

So, when Eve responded to the serpent, she unwittingly entered into a conversation with someone against whom she was no match.

But the serpent said to the woman, "You will not surely die. For God knows that when you eat of it your eyes will be opened, and you will be like God, knowing good and evil" (Genesis 3:5 ESV).

4

Here is where he seized the moment to give his own version of the truth, and she swallowed the bait: "Yes, the wise serpent was right. What's the harm in trying?"

So when the woman saw that the tree was good for food, and that it was a delight to the eyes, and that the tree was to be desired to make one wise, she took of its fruit and ate, and she also gave some to her husband who was with her, and he ate. Then the eyes of both were opened, and they knew that they were naked. And they sewed fig leaves together and made themselves loincloths (Genesis 3:6-7 ESV).

So now they had to bear the consequences of their failure to listen to the One who gave the command.

And they heard the sound of the LORD God walking in the garden in the cool of the day, and the man and his wife hid themselves from the presence of the Lord God among the trees of the garden (Genesis 3:8 ESV).

They hid. When we don't listen—in other words, when we don't heed the "God said"—we go into hiding. And why do we hide? Adam and Eve were trying to protect themselves from God. But we don't ever have to protect ourselves from God because God is not the problem. Our not keeping the "God said" is the problem.

Another example of a person hearing but not listening or obeying was Lot's wife. We find this account in Genesis 19. As Lot's family was fleeing Sodom from the wrath of God, they were told not to look back. Lot's wife heard the warning not to look back, but she did not listen. Because of her failure to heed the instructions, she looked back at the place she was departing from and became a pillar of salt (See Genesis 19:26).

We have to stop looking back with longing and nostalgia at the situation God is bringing us out of! Purpose in your heart to come out of that place. Cut yourself loose from those companions, those thoughts, and those habits. Sometimes you may not feel like you are being brought out, but God is delivering you from your own destruction.

Your Moment Is Here

I want you to catch something important here. God does not wait until you come out to tell you your freedom is upon you. He does not wait until it is in your hands to tell you the door is open. The door is open; the way has been cleared. It is your season, your time, your blessing. It may not even look like it, but do not go on thinking that it doesn't look like the thing God

> *Listen to the point that you trust God, and walk by faith, not by sight.*

said. Instead, act on what God dropped directly into your spirit.

So, God just spoke something over your life. You heard it, but did you listen? Respond to what has been spoken. Praise Him for your new season—your liberty, your deliverance! Stop praising based on what you see. Praise Him based on what He is saying here and now ... because you've caught it. You don't even see a door opening with your natural eyes or a way being made. You can't see how you're going to come out of your circumstances, but in your spirit, you feel God is saying you are coming out, being delivered, and being set free.

To further illustrate this, the children of Israel had a report of what the Promised Land looked like—a land of abundance but also a land of fortified cities inhabited by giants (See Numbers 13). It was a contradictory report. But God, through Joshua and Caleb kept saying, "It is yours; take it right now! This is your hour. I've released it into your life. I am doing it now. The blessing is yours now." But, because of the fear put upon them by the other ten spies, they found every excuse for not moving into the land of promise. They put all their limiting and narrow perceptions on God. Stop putting your limitations on God! What's a limitation for you is an opportunity for God.

Why are you saying, "It can't be!" when *God* said, "It is! It's yours! You have it now! It's done! Take it!" Listen for what God is saying to you in this season. Listen and not just hear. Listen to the point that you can see it in your spirit, and then it is as good as done. Listen to the point that you trust God, and walk by faith, not by sight. Listen and obey.

There are myriad voices trying to tell the church what to do today, but they are setting up barriers and distractions to what God actually said. The adversary with his many voices is trying to pollute the church through our thoughts and our hearing ability. However, the one voice that must prevail is the voice of the Lord.

Calls to Prayer

One of the most crucial things the Lord told the church to do is to *"pray unceasingly"* (1 Thessalonians 5:17). We have all heard it—but are we listening? Are we spiritually inattentive like the children of Israel were at the threshold of the Promised Land?

Are we attentively, actively, and obediently listening to the Lord's call for us to pray?

There are several calls to prayer in Scripture:

Pray persistently:

And he spake a parable unto them to this end, that men ought always to pray, and not to faint ... (Luke 18:1)

Pray without ceasing:

Pray without ceasing. In every thing give thanks: for this is the will of God in Christ Jesus concerning you (1 Thessalonians 5:17-18).

Pray in the secret place:

But thou, when thou prayest, enter into thy closet, and when thou hast shut thy door, pray to thy Father which is in secret; and thy Father which seeth in secret shall reward thee openly (Matthew 6:6).

Pray for your nation, community, family, and loved ones:

If my people, which are called by my name, shall humble themselves, and pray, and seek my face, and turn from their wicked ways; then will I hear from heaven, and will forgive their sin, and will heal their land (2 Chronicles 7:14).

Did you hear that? Are you listening? When you pray and repent for the sins of the land—the people, the leaders, the government—God not only forgives their sins but heals the land.

With so many serious and urgent calls to prayer, it can become our purpose as a company of believers. Prayer can become continuous. The potential for us to pray is here right now. It is inside of you now. You can talk to God and make your request; you can intercede for others; and you can pray in the Spirit. You don't have to pray eloquently with the mannerisms of some great intercessors, or of your pastor or leader. You just pray the way God gives you to pray as led by the Spirit.

Now, not everybody may be listening and obeying the call to prayer, but the church has to pray. We have to listen and obey the command to pray ... because we are different from the world. We are a people that move by faith, not by sight.

Challenges for the Church

The church is a community of faith-filled believers whose head is Jesus Christ (See Colossians 1:18). Essentially, it is His church. As the body of Christ on earth whose members are filled with the Holy Ghost, the church has been called out from the world to serve God. Moreover, the church has great power and authority as Jesus declares in Matthew 16:18:

And I say also unto thee, That thou art Peter, and upon this rock I will build my church; and the gates of hell shall not prevail against it.

Jesus said He was going to build the church, and the Greek word for "build" here, _oikodomēsō_, means "to strengthen." Not only did He say He was going to build the church, but He also promised to strengthen and edify it. The work in the church He is doing is a continuous process, so the church is always in process.

We all know the church is not perfect, so we have to stop trying to make it perfect as soon as we join. Stop abandoning the church because of the faults and shortcomings. The Lord is building the church and He knows what it takes to build it, for it to be sustained and to thrive, and to continue from one generation to the next. He knows how to keep the church from dying as we can see from the way He addressed the seven churches in Revelation 2 and 3 about their most vulnerable areas.

Your local church may be recently formed, or it may have been standing for decades or centuries. The only reason that your church and the churches worldwide have survived is that the Lord has committed Himself to building the church. He said the gates of hell are not going to prevail, not going to overpower, not going to dominate, not going to defeat the church, for the church has this great strength in that it is the Lord who is building it!

Today the church worldwide faces many obstacles and challenges, but the Lord knows how to build His church. And for every child of God, when you are in your bad season, just understand He is using all the negative elements to build you. He is using the opposition to make you stronger and take you higher. All of this works together for a purpose:

> And we know that all things work together for good to them that love God, to them who are the called according to his purpose (Romans 8:28).

> But the God of all grace, who hath called us unto his eternal glory by Christ Jesus, after that ye have suffered a while, make you perfect, stablish, strengthen, settle you (1 Peter 5:10).

After you've had your hard time, look at what is coming out of your "going through" period. The Lord is going to *perfect* you—that means "restore" and "equip" you. If you allow God to work while you are in your "going through" season, He will equip you for greater success and victory. He will establish you, meaning "confirm" you, and "make you more able and capable." Aren't you thankful for that?

So, when you come out of what you are going through now, you are going to be more anointed and more on fire. You are going to be more capable and have more resources within you. You are going to have more of the power of God working through you to accomplish His purpose. Not only that, He is going to strengthen you and increase your resolve. And, after you've gone through this series of trials, there is going to be a fierce determination on the inside of you where the enemy once used to hinder you and hold you back. The enemy will try to hit you and block you, but there's going to be a pressing and resolve in you pushing him back, resisting him. And there is more. God says that as you go through, He is also settling you. You may have been on shaky ground, but now He is going to set you down on a solid foundation. He knows what the church needs: to be built up and to be strengthened.

The church today has been described in many ways. Some describe it as lazy, tired, closed, hypocritical, insignificant, and no longer relevant. Some say the church has become mega, but it is silent, a sleeping giant. Other people say the church is kind, generous, prosperous, and fulfilling its call. Some of these things are accurate, and some are outright wrong. But we are still missing something: prayer.

Few seem to recognize that the church has to pray. Prayer is our lifeline. We need to pray because prayer works. Will you be one of the few who recognize our desperate need to pray? I hope so!

Living by Faith

There is a story about prayer worth sharing. Back in the 1800s, a couple by the name of the Muellers, a husband-and-wife missionary team, was called by God to work with orphans. They ministered to thousands of children and built several homes. They funded their ministry, not by donations, or having a series of concerts or crusades. None of that! They built their ministry solely on prayer, totally trusting in the Lord for provision. Their prayer was constant; it was their mainstay.

So, they prayed for God to touch the hearts of donors that would provide for the orphans. One morning when there was absolutely no food, Mr. Mueller told the children to set the table. The table was set—empty bowls, empty plates, empty cups—but

> *We need to pray because prayer works.*

it was set. Do you have the faith to set the table? He called the children to gather and take a seat at the table. They took their seats and Mr. Mueller prayed. Will you pray at an empty table? He blessed the food that was not there, the plates that had no food, and the cups that had nothing to drink in them.

When he finished praying, there was a knock at the door. It was the baker saying, "I got up early this morning and it was on my heart to bring bread to the orphanage." And they had all the bread they needed. Then the milkman with his cart going down the street also stopped by. His cart had broken down right in front of the orphanage where they'd been praying and he said, "I can't let this milk spoil." Of all the doors on the street, it was Mueller's door he knocked on and told him, "Here is the milk ready for you." In this moment and season of your life, I encourage you to set your table. That is, place your needs before the Lord, pray and thank Him in advance, and then wait on the Lord. Finally, be spiritually sensitive to His answer, and bless Him for what He does and says. Church, if you want a knock on your door, you have to pray.

Why Come Boldly?

Hebrews 4:15 gives us this assurance: *"For we have not an high priest which cannot be touched with the feeling of our infirmities; but was in all points tempted like as we are, yet without sin."* As our High Priest, Jesus knows our weaknesses because He's been there. He sympathizes and understands. He knows that many times it is out of our infirmities and pressing lack that we pray.

This is His instruction to the church:

Let us therefore come boldly unto the throne of grace, that we may obtain mercy, and find grace to help in time of need (Hebrews 4:16).

"Come boldly" means "come directly with confidence, honesty, and with courage, regardless of the circumstances."

You can come to Him with all your inadequacies, knowing He is mighty, powerful, and able to do the impossible.

Grace is "favor from Him that we do not deserve."

Our "time of need" (Greek *ĕukairŏs*) is a *kairos* time, "a favorable or well-timed occasion;" it is our breakthrough moment.

To "obtain mercy" is to "find grace, favor, kindness." The Lord wants to release His kindness upon us every time we approach Him in prayer. So, present yourself at the throne, knowing He is able to do exceedingly abundantly above all you could ever ask or think (See Ephesians 3:20). Stop putting barriers and limitations on God, for God can move in spite of you.

We don't need another corporate prayer meeting to be scheduled just because we have corporate prayer on our program. What we want is faith that what we are doing works. Are you discovering that, no matter how much time we schedule, if prayer is not in you, you are not going to pray … even if you go through the motions of prayer?

Only the effective fervent prayer of the righteous avails much (See James 5:16).

But even in our weaknesses, there is mercy for us. We have God's favor and kindness. We can find grace and help in fulfilling our needs. We don't always know what the need is, but if we can get in prayer, the Holy Ghost has a way of just starting us by saying, "Help, Lord, rescue, support, and supply whatever is needed."

As we decide to be more committed to prayer, I have a proposition. My proposition is not only for the men or women in ministry, the trustees, the ministry directors, the deacons or the ushers, the admin, the mothers, or the children, it is for all of us. We are the Body. We are the Church, and we must pray.

Prayer is a powerful resource, but it is our responsibility to use it, activate it, take advantage of it, and push through. There is a call to prayer, and things happen when we pray. The church must hear and listen to that call. Prayer is on the inside of you. Take a moment and remember how a dying thief prayed his last prayer as he hung on the cross and found eternal life! Always keep in mind that God has given the church authority and power in prayer.

End of Chapter Reflection

What scripture in this chapter resonated with you the most? Why?

_____

_____

_____

_____

_____

_____

List at least three key principles provided in this chapter.

1. _____

_____

2. _____

_____

3. _____

_____

How will your prayer life change based on the principles presented in this chapter?

_____

_____

_____

_____

_____

_____

Prayer Time: Write a prayer asking God to help you apply the principles you have learned from this chapter.

_____

_____

_____

_____

_____

_____

_____

_____

CHAPTER TWO

Walk in Authority
and Power

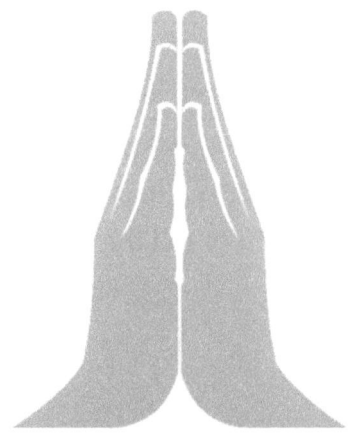

The early church walked in authority and power. They saw amazing signs and wonders, and thousands were added to their number each day. At the same time, the church suffered tremendous persecution with believers hounded by the authorities on all sides. Nevertheless, they bravely soldiered on—on their knees. Although this was a fledgling church, it had enormous power.

For Christ had said, "...*where two or three are gathered together in my name, there am I in the midst of them*" (Matthew 18:20) and He had given them all authority and power to make disciples of all nations (Matthew 28:18).

Peter's Imprisonment

In Acts 12 we find that Herod had Peter put in prison: "... *but prayer was made without ceasing of the church unto God for him*" (Acts 12:5, emphasis added).

Notice that the prayer was made "without ceasing" by "the church" of Jesus Christ. Just as Peter was continually held in prison, the church remained enduring in prayer.

As prayer for Peter went up, miraculously, he was led out of the prison by angels without the knowledge of the guards. Peter found his way to the house where the intercessors were gathered. As Peter knocked on the gate, he was met by a girl, who in her excitement left him outside as she ran in to tell the others. No one believed her:

And they said unto her, Thou art mad. But she constantly affirmed that it was even so. Then said they, It is his angel. But Peter continued knocking: and when they had opened the door, and saw him, they were astonished (Acts 12:15-16).

Bless their hearts! They were so "unceasing" in their prayer that they did not realize that the answer had already come—and was standing at the gate!

The Power of the Church

So, in Acts 12, the church prays. But who is the church? The church is people, not a building. The Greek word for church is *ekklēsia*, in other words, the "called out ones." The church is a community of believers who have put their faith in Jesus, totally depending on Him for their salvation.

Now, not everybody makes up the church—not everybody who shows up on a Sunday morning, whether online or in person. No, only those who follow Jesus, trust in Jesus, and have received Jesus as their *personal* Lord and Savior are the church.

Your parents and grandparents may have received Him as Lord, but if you want to join the ranks of the called-out ones, you must receive Him and seek Him for yourself.

At the time of Acts 12, the church was young but vibrant because the people prayed. It was facing constant persecution, but they were resilient because they prayed.

The apostle Paul describes the situation vividly:

We are troubled on every side, yet not distressed; we are perplexed, but not in despair; Persecuted, but not forsaken; cast down, but not destroyed (2 Corinthians 4:8-9).

The New Living Translation says:

We are pressed on every side by troubles, but we are not crushed. We are perplexed, but not driven to despair. We are hunted down, but never abandoned by God. We get knocked down, but we are not destroyed.

The above passage is loaded with encouragement for the church. The explosive promise here is God never abandons us! God does not neglect or leave us. Again, no matter what we, as the church, are going through, we, too, are not abandoned by God or destroyed. That is why we praise Him in the midst of it all, in spite of it all, and through it all. Even when we stumble and get out of line, He never forsakes us.

Let that soak in our spirits: God never abandons or deserts us. He is never unfaithful to us; He never departs from us; and He never neglects us. He is always caring, always loving, and always concerned about us. Even when we are out of His will in our

> *God never abandons or deserts us.*

disobedience and rebellion, He still loves us and sticks with us. For Him to abandon us is unthinkable. Just as He said to

Joshua, He is saying to us, *"I will never leave you nor forsake you"* (Joshua 1:5 NIV). Oh, the blessings of being in the church are countless!

Still, many of us are going through severe challenges right now. We don't talk about it because everybody around us is going through much the same thing. We are just holding it inside. But, remember, the only reason we haven't cracked up and lost it all is that God has been with us all along. We would never have made it if He had left us to our own resources. And so, we lift our hands saying, "Lord, we bless You! We give You glory! We honor You!"

The church in Peter and Paul's day kept their faith in Him. They clearly understood they could count on God. With all that was working against them, the church had power from on high. Evil may be working against you, even over time, but no matter how much you're going through, because you are in the body of Christ, and because you belong to Him, always remember you have power and His presence. You are part of His church.

When the enemy is working against you, make sure you have power from on high. Remember what Jesus promised His church in Acts 1:8:

> *But ye shall receive power, after that the Holy Ghost is come upon you: and ye shall be witnesses unto me both in Jerusalem, and in all Judaea, and in Samaria, and unto the uttermost part of the earth.*

This is *dunamis power*. Dunamis power is the supernatural ability that He has placed in you, and that includes the ability to pray. You have the ability, the might, the strength, the miracle-working power, and the persistence to keep praying in spite of all your setbacks and disappointments.

The Beginning of Revival

This dunamis power was not released at a board meeting or at a concert, or even a revival meeting or a big convention. The power was not released by making a traditional oath; it wasn't by following some formula or order of worship to bring on the anointing. No, none of that: the power was released in prayer.

It started in an upper room in Jerusalem.

And when they were come in, they went up into an upper room, where abode both Peter, and James, and John, and Andrew, Philip, and Thomas, Bartholomew, and Matthew, James the son of Alphaeus, and Simon Zelotes, and Judas the brother of James. These all continued with one accord in prayer and supplication, with the women, and Mary the mother of Jesus, and with his brethren (Acts 1:13-14).

In the above, note the word "abode," which means "stayed put." It was more than staying put in the upper room or in each other's company. It means they were staying put in prayer. They were not quitting. They were planted in prayer and prayer was planted in them. They continued with one accord. Everyone's mind was in the same place. Their thoughts were not scattered. They prayed with one accord—they all agreed on the following: "We're going to pray for strength, for endurance, for boldness. We're going to resist." Can we all agree that we are going to pray together and that we are going to pray the same thing?

That prayer in the upper room worked. Power was released. They were effectively praying in the next chapter—Acts 2:1-4:

And when the day of Pentecost was fully come, they were all with one accord in one place. And suddenly there came a sound from heaven as of a rushing mighty wind, and it filled all the house where they were sitting. And there appeared unto them cloven tongues like as of fire, and it sat upon each of them. And they were all filled with the Holy Ghost, and began to speak with other tongues, as the Spirit gave them utterance (Acts 2:1-4).

They were filled with the Holy Ghost (not with gossip or fear-mongering). "The Spirit gave them utterance"—that heavenly prayer language came spontaneously because the Holy Spirit fell. They went around praising God, telling of His wondrous acts, and extolling His name before an amazed crowd.

These were trying times for the emerging church. Throughout chapter 12, the church was facing animosity and hostility, hatred and bitterness, rejection and cold hearts because of their relationship, faith, and commitment to the Lord Jesus Christ. The persecution escalated with Herod Agrippa, who wanted to seek more favor from the Jews. He had already killed James, the brother of John, son of Zebedee, and disciple of Jesus. Then he proceeded to arrest Peter. Who was going to be next?

At this point, they were helpless in the natural. There was no social or political system available to them to come to their aid. So, they did what they knew to do—pray. No doubt some of them felt worn out and distressed. Nevertheless, they prayed in the midst of the wickedness that was coming upon them because of their call to preach the Gospel.

The proof that their prayer worked before encouraged them to pray now even more. When the religious authorities threatened the disciples with further punishment if they continued to preach the Gospel, they answered with boldness and even preached to them:

Then Peter and the other apostles answered and said, We ought to obey God rather than men. The God of our fathers raised up Jesus, whom ye slew and hanged on a tree. Him hath God exalted with his right hand to be a Prince and a Saviour, for to give repentance to Israel, and forgiveness of sins. And we are his witnesses of these things; and so is also the Holy Ghost, whom God hath given to them that obey him (Acts 5:29-32).

No wonder miracles followed everywhere they went! On the day of Pentecost three thousand souls were saved … and continued by the thousands each day. It was through prayer that the man lame from birth was healed at the temple gate. In Acts 4, the church prayed for strength in dealing with their enemy, and the place was shaken and their strength was restored.

Philip, the evangelist, shared the Gospel with the Ethiopian eunuch from the court of Queen Candace and that nobleman took the Gospel to his own nation. Saul had an encounter with Jesus Christ on the Damascus Road, which turned his life around. Cornelius, the centurion, and his entire household was saved. Philip brought salvation and deliverance to Samaria. Peter's shadow healed sick people as it fell on them in the streets. The dead were raised. The church grew and the Gospel spread throughout the Roman Empire. In all of this success and victory, the church knew the driving force was prayer. If the church is going to continue in this vain of success, we must pray.

Listen and Obey

As for you, child of God, your goal is not just to hear yourself when you pray, but also to listen out for the Lord's instruction. This is what young Samuel did when he heard the Lord's voice calling him from his bed at the door of the temple, *"Speak; for thy servant heareth"* (1 Samuel 3:10). In effect, little Samuel was saying, "Lord, I am ready to receive what You're saying. I'm ready to obey. I am submitting to Your authority. I am listening. You have my undivided attention."

You see, listening goes beyond hearing: its intent is to follow through in obedience. Too many of us claim we are listening, but we are missing the element of obedience. The apostle James insists: *"Therefore to him that knoweth to do good, and doeth it not, to him it is sin"* (James 4:17, emphasis added).

> ...*listening goes beyond hearing: its intent is to follow through in obedience.*

The apostle James tells us that listening is revealed by two things: knowing and doing. Knowing means being aware of the facts and the role you are asked to play. But, more importantly, the information is now embedded, planted, and rooted in you. And then, doing it is carrying out the command that is already in you. You are producing the behavior.

Sadly, some of us are not praying because prayer is not in us; it is not part of our make-up. And when we do not pray, we are unaware of the corresponding action required of us. All too often, we end up in horrible situations simply because we did not know...because we did not listen. We must listen because the call to prayer is seen throughout the

Bible. There is a definite call in the word of God for us to pray ceaselessly, in all circumstances.

Prayer is a powerful weapon, stronger than any invisible enemy that can come against your life.

For the weapons of our warfare are not carnal, but mighty through God to the pulling down of strong holds (2 Corinthians 10:4).

Our enemy is not people but invisible powers of darkness (See Ephesians 6:12). Prayer has the capacity to dismantle the places where these powers have set up camp. Prayer is a vital part of our spiritual armor because it helps mobilize and lubricate all six weapons and helps them function in unison. We can't serve in the kingdom without using the weapon of prayer.

How to Pray

So, what is prayer? One of the Greek words for prayer is *proseuche,* meaning turn all of yourself and your attention towards God. In addition, it means "to lift your request to God." At the most basic level, it is to talk to God. Did you talk to Him this morning and will you end the day talking to Him? Do you talk to Him in your natural authentic voice and share your thoughts with Him as you would with a friend?

So how do we pray? Take your cue from Jesus. When the disciples asked how to pray, He gave these instructions:

And it came to pass, that, as he was praying in a certain place, when he ceased, one of his disciples said unto him, Lord, teach us to pray, as John also taught his disciples.

And he said unto them, When ye pray, say, Our Father which art in heaven, Hallowed be thy name. Thy kingdom come. Thy will be done, as in heaven, so in earth. Give us day by day our daily bread. And forgive us our sins; for we also forgive every one that is indebted to us. And lead us not into temptation; but deliver us from evil (Luke 11:1-4).

Jesus showed us this pattern of prayer. First, He addresses God as "Father." God is our Father, too. This means we have a personal relationship with the Almighty God and can come to Him as His children. Next, we hallow His name, by honoring Him in living holy lives and giving Him all the glory and honor, praise and worship. When we say, "Thy kingdom come, Thy will be done," we are proclaiming His Lordship over all the nations and ourselves. We are declaring that every tribe and tongue will bow to the name of Jesus in complete obedience and submission (See Philippians 2:10-11). Then we ask for our daily bread, believing that all our material and spiritual needs will be met.

Finally, we ask for forgiveness for our sins. No matter how serious they are, we come believing that they are forgiven according to 1 John 1:9. And just as we are forgiven, we forgive all those who have wronged us. We forgive them unconditionally as many times as they have sinned just as the Lord has been so gracious to us. If we hold back someone's sin and refuse to forgive, we are putting ourselves in the hands of the tormentors that Jesus describes in Matthew 18:34. Who are the tormentors? Sickness, guilt, a troubled mind, a hardened heart, in anyone who harbors unforgiveness. And, once we have forgiveness, we ask to be delivered from all the temptations of the evil one.

When we pray according to this prayer, we commit to following the instructions within it to honor God and be His vessel of peace.

Amid all the unrest in the world and the deployment of sophisticated weapons of war, we have the greatest weapon: the power of prayer. It releases the protection, the power, and the love of the Father over our lives and all those within our sphere of influence. It dismantles the plans and schemes of the enemy. It brings healing and hope.

I want to relate an incident to show the love of the Father to us as we pray in obedience. My wife and I were coming home from the hospital. My wife was in tears after bidding her beloved father goodbye. Seeing a missed call on her phone, she called the person back. The person had not yet heard about the passing of my wife's father and began to lay out to her a crisis in their own family.

As I drove, I observed my wife wiping her tears, hardly able to compose herself. I saw her put aside her own needs for a few minutes and begin to pray with the person whose loved one had been placed on a ventilator.

Through all the heartbreak, pain, and concern, we have a mighty weapon. I heard my wife, with her sanctified self, pray until the other person on the line began to feel lifted up and hopeful.

Let us get serious about prayer. Let the foolishness, the animosity, and the defeat go, and let us pray. Do you need a miracle today? Do you need strength or help? Do you need direction? Do you need calmness or assurance? Let us pray. Prayer works!

End of Chapter Reflection

What scripture in this chapter resonated with you the most? Why?

_____

_____

_____

_____

_____

_____

List at least three key principles from this chapter.

1. _____

_____

2. _____

_____

3. _____

_____

How will your prayer life change based on the principles presented in this chapter?

_____

_____

_____

_____

_____

_____

Prayer Time: Write a prayer asking God to help you apply the principles you have learned from this chapter.

_____

_____

_____

_____

_____

_____

_____

_____

CHAPTER THREE

Keep Your Focus

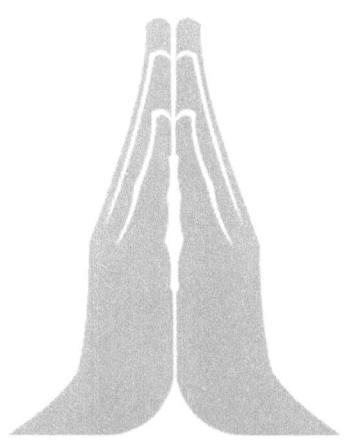

I drive my granddaughter to school Monday through Friday. Our 20-minute journey includes morning devotion. She knows it as she puts on her seat belt and gets her devotional book and Bible. After reading, comes a simple but specific question from me, "So what did you learn from this morning's devotion?"

Most of the time, my granddaughter gives this wonderful response. I'm actually amazed at her recall and her application of Scripture to life. However, there are times I get this blank look, "Oh no! I'm confused! I don't understand!" These are the times that she may have heard but did not listen. She may not have been focused on what was read. So, I have to ask probing questions to help her refocus and move up to the listening realm. Some of us need to also move up to the listening realm.

Staying Spiritually Focused

The Lord knows when we are losing our spiritual focus or when it is being challenged, how to speak to our spiritual focus. This is what He did with a ruler of the synagogue named Jairus who was bringing Jesus to minister to his dying daughter.

When Jairus told Jesus his daughter was at the point of death (See Mark 5:23), he was communicating her extremely serious condition. This thing was about to take her to a conclusion, and He was saying, "I don't like the conclusion that I see."

Have you ever found yourself in a similar pattern where you say, "I don't like where this is going either"? Jairus had just seen how the woman with the issue of blood was miraculously healed because she had put her faith and focus on Jesus (See Mark 5:25-29). Jairus, too, was trying to do the same thing—keep his mind on Jesus and stay spiritually focused.

You see, when we are spiritually focused, we are putting our mind on Jesus:

Looking unto Jesus the author and finisher of our faith; who for the joy that was set before him endured the cross, despising the shame, and is set down at the right hand of the throne of God (Hebrews 12:2).

Writing this when the church was really going through tough times, the apostle Paul told them, "Look unto Jesus!" Jesus was not distracted by the pain of the cross but kept His eyes on the joy of winning us into His kingdom. We, too, when we pray in our tough situations, should look to Jesus. Our attention is not diverted. We are not distracted because we have put aside our preoccupations so that we can see Jesus.

We, too, when we pray in our tough situations, should look to Jesus.

Oftentimes, I have to be intentional in my thinking about Jesus and tell myself, "You're going to put your mind on

Jesus. You're going to think about His wonder, think about His might, think about His power, think about His glory, and think about His love and faithfulness."

Jairus had experienced the presence of the Lord. But have you? That's why you need to worship not just in church, but also at home. Worship ushers in the presence of the Lord. If you are a worship leader, you will have an easier time leading in worship if you had worshiped before arriving at church. But if all our worship is dependent on when we get there, we are going to have to work diligently to lift the atmosphere. May God take us to the place where our worship is not about who is up in front of us, who is leading the song, but Who we are worshiping.

Jairus knew that the Lord's presence makes seemingly impossible things possible. If you understand the magnitude and power of His presence, things can happen that you did not even ask for—because He is there. Things can turn around because you did not give up. His presence makes things possible because you have hope.

Jairus knew the potential of the Lord's presence. Things were going one way, but Jesus was with him. However, before Jesus and Jairus could get to the house, the dreaded news came (See Mark 5:35). For Jairus, the thought came, "I was trying to keep this from happening, but it still happened." They sent word to Jairus not to trouble the Master because it was too late. His daughter had died.

How many times have we felt like it's too late? That's only because of our limited perspective. But I want you to know the Lord can always do something. Even if He did not do what you preferred Him to do, we have to develop the mindset that He can do something new and powerful each time.

It is very clear from the context of, *"Why troublest thou the Master any further?"* that they were speaking to Jairus and did not want Jesus to hear. What I want you to know is that no one can keep anything from Jesus. He hears everything that was spoken against you, spoken behind your back, spoken to bring you down and discourage you. And, when things get to their worst stage, Jesus does not initially respond to what we heard—the bad news, the terrible situation. His initial response is to *you*.

Jairus, as his hope dimmed, was starting to lose his focus. The potential miracle that comes with the Lord's presence was starting to slip away. But Jesus was getting him back to his focus spiritually.

As soon as Jesus heard the word that was spoken, he saith unto the ruler of the synagogue, Be not afraid, only believe (Mark 5:36).

"He saith unto the ruler ..." He spoke not to the ones who brought the bad news, but He spoke to the one who saw the potential in Jesus.

"Jesus, what did you say?"

"Be not afraid, only believe," He said to the ruler of the synagogue. This is a charge not to be moved by fear. This is not the time to be overwhelmed by the news you just heard.

You may have just gotten the worst news of your life. But He is here to tell you, "Be not afraid; only believe." Have faith in Jesus who is with you.

You say, "The thing that I did not want to see happen just did," but He says, "Be not afraid; only believe."

You need only two things to get your spiritual focus back, one, "Be not afraid," and two, "Only believe."

Jesus is speaking directly to Jairus, not the crowd. Others are milling around, but this word is for Jairus. Have you ever gone to church and just knew that the word of the Lord coming through the person ministering was directly for you?

What is Jesus saying? He's saying, "I'm commanding you, Jairus, for your own good, do not get stuck in this pattern of being anxious. Do not be apprehensive and terrified. Just trust Me!"

Do not allow your negative emotions to determine your next step. You cannot make productive calls for your life when you are messed up emotionally. Jesus is calling for you to know that He is greater than what you are facing. He is greater than the fiery darts that are coming against you. He is greater than the cause of your pain.

"For the Lord most high is terrible," says Psalm 47:2— "terrible" in the sense of "awesome." When life is not at its best, you can still say, "God is awesome. He is to be honored because He is the One who has the authority."

Great is the Lord, and greatly to be praised in the city of our God, in the mountain of his holiness (Psalm 48:1).

So, praise Him in His holiness. Praise Him for releasing us from our burdens.

When the Lord turned again the captivity of Zion, we were like them that dream (Psalm 126:1). Focused prayer and faith will transform your nightmare.

Revive that Dream

The Lord is true to His word. He knows how to smooth out the messy pieces of your life and turn your nightmare back into your dream. So do not let your mind get stuck in a nightmare. Speak out God's promise. "Lord, you promised to give me my dream. I declare that dream is about to become a reality!" I once went through some trouble when I slipped right back into doubt, but God turned me around in my dream. Are you ready for your dream to come to pass? It is *focus* that brings you back to your dream. Start dreaming again.

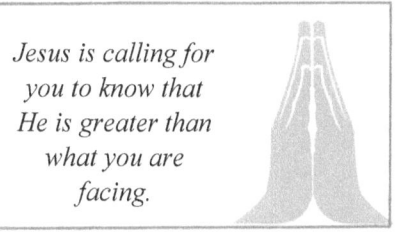

Jesus is calling for you to know that He is greater than what you are facing.

I come against every spirit that is trying to block your dream. I come against every demonic force trying to close your eyes to a dream. You have been having that dream for a long time, and I come against the dream killer in the name of Jesus!

Then was our mouth filled with laughter (indicating joy and happiness), and our tongue with singing: then said they among the heathen, The Lord hath done great things for them (Psalm 126:2, emphasis added).

This was the cry of the children of Israel when they were finally released from captivity. They thought it was all their imagination. Then their mouth was filled with laughter when they saw it was real.

When you come out of your nightmare, and lock into your dream, look for the appropriate response. Not only is there laughter but your tongue is filled with singing. Sing in your car; sing on the job. Break forth into singing! Why are you singing? It is because the Lord has done great things for you, too.

So, let us celebrate. Not only celebrate, but, like the children of Israel, we are going to proclaim, "The Lord has done great things for me! For He is great and He does great things!"

How great is our God, sing with me
How great is our God, and all will see
How great, how great is our God!

End of Chapter Reflection

What scripture in this chapter resonated with you the most?
Why?

_____

_____

_____

_____

_____

_____

List at least three key principles from this chapter.

1. _____

_____

2. _____

_____

3. _____

_____

How will your prayer life change based on the principles presented in this chapter?

_____

_____

_____

_____

_____

_____

Prayer Time: Write a prayer asking God to help you apply the principles you have learned from this chapter.

_____

_____

_____

_____

_____

_____

_____

_____

CHAPTER FOUR

Refocus Your Ear

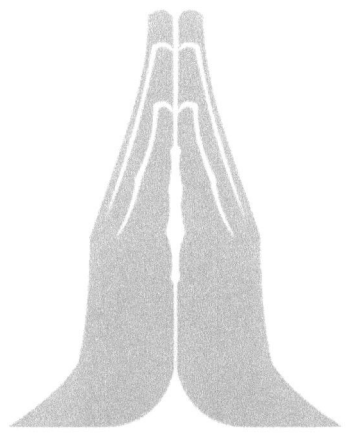

Bad news has a way of shaking your foundation, shattering your dream, and threatening to muffle your listening ear. When you receive bad news or you are surrounded by negativity, it is hard to hear God speak. You want to hear Him, but the other voices threaten to drown out His voice.

In a previous chapter, we saw how Jairus had to get his spiritual ears back into alignment after hearing the terrible news about his daughter. But Jesus challenged Jairus to listen to His voice that spoke life into the situation. All of us find ourselves in the same struggle from time to time, and then we are challenged to hear Jesus above the bad news. That is what the refocus is all about. It's about listening to Jesus no matter what's going on around us.

Remember what Jesus told Jairus as He saw him struggling with his emotions: *"As soon as Jesus heard the word that was spoken, he saith unto the ruler of the synagogue, Be not afraid, only believe"* (Mark 5:36). One, don't be afraid. Two, only believe. These two postures are essential in getting your spiritual focus back. You do it, not after things are over; no, the real assignment is to get your spiritual ears reset when you are going through the fire. Do not be afraid. Only believe.

He's Able

Jesus is calling for the Jairuses of this world to know that He is greater than anything we could ever face. Whether the challenges bring change for the better or not, the thought has to be ingrained in us that He's great. When we say the Lord is great, we are saying He is awesome, He is honorable, He is remarkable, He is out of the ordinary, He is powerful, He is strong and mighty, He is able to do far more than we expect!

Now unto him that is able to do exceeding abundantly above all that we ask or think, according to the power that worketh in us (Ephesians 3:20).

You do not have to wait until the greatness is manifested. Right in the trying moment, you can praise Him because He is great and He is able. That must be rooted in our spirit. It cannot be based on our experience, or what we are dealing with, or how things turn out. Whether it turns out the way we like or not, the Lord is still great.

So, when we go into prayer, we must enter with the mindset that God can do what we are asking, He is able, He is sufficient, and He has the power. We do not have to have Him and something else as well. No! He is sufficient to meet ALL of our needs. He can do it without our help.

Recognize that the enemy wants us to get locked into problem mode, fixed on our ordeal, our dilemma, and our complication. He wants us to see nothing but the forces pressing in against us. But here is Jesus calling us to focus on Him and who He is – to move up into the listening realm.

Will you take a moment to tune in to Him right now? Will you see Him above your circumstances, above the situation, above the conditions and the facts of the case you are facing?

Be honest with yourself. It is true, you often face many challenges that do not make sense because they are painful, irritating, hurtful, and beyond what you deserve. But, regardless of how bad it looks, the Lord wants us to move up and listen to Him, especially to His call to pray. And though He can call you to pray at the strangest of times, did He not say through Paul the apostle: *"Pray without ceasing. In every thing give thanks: for this is the will of God in Christ Jesus concerning you"* (1 Thessalonians 5:17-18)?

Pray All the Time

Now, although it is good to have a set routine, prayer is not limited to a prescribed place, hour, or number of times per day. I know of a vast and growing world religion that tells you to pray five times a day. But here in the scripture, there is no limit to the number of times or where we ought to pray—you do not have to face a certain direction to pray either. Prayer should be a constant component of our daily lives, and any place in which we are led to pray is the right place. We can come boldly to His throne of grace each time, knowing with confidence that we are praying to God, our Father, and He desires to give us grace and help (Hebrews 4:16).

Again, because we are in a relationship, we do not need to use prayer to manipulate God, put Him in a corner, box Him in, or tell Him why He has to do something. Simply pray because you trust Him as your Father.

And pray to give Him thanks in all circumstances. If it is good, thank Him. If it is bad, thank Him as well because He is sovereign. He is in control, He can turn around any situation, and He can cause us to triumph (to win, to have victory, to have success) in any adversity. Even if it gets worse, tell yourself you're going to win.

As mentioned previously, we should not pray aloud only when we have an audience of people because the truth is, your real audience is God, not people. Therefore, pray in your private place and the God who hears you in secret will reward you openly (See Matthew 6:6).

In Acts 12, we saw the church moving in step with God's instructions because they had tapped into the listening realm. Prayer

> ...prayer is not limited to a prescribed place, hour, or number of times per day.

was in them. They were persecuted by the authorities, but with prayer, they learned to override their fear, frustration, uncertainty, and discouragement. When sudden attacks came upon them, they retreated to their secret place. They were not praying out of religious ritual but out of believing in God and, from their experience of Jesus, knowing that He cares. Their praying proves that they did not just hear, but they also listened to what God was speaking in the moment. We, too, trust Him because we are in a relationship with Him. We pray knowing He cares and is in control.

In the seasons coming upon the church today, we had better step up our prayer. Pray with our regular groups during the week, show up at our special prayer meetings, and pray during alerts especially as you see greater darkness approaching. We have to pray corporately and pray alone in our personal prayer time.

Power and Authority

The early church of Acts 12 had particular characteristics that demonstrated their power and authority. They were not governed by worldly values. They were not intimidated by the authorities concerning their primary call to preach the Gospel. They showed love and concern, compassion and care, especially for the needy. They had faith. They had praise and worship. All this contributed to their power, spiritual power from on high. This power gave victory and strength and caused people to overcome and find hope. It was, in a word, life-transforming power.

Jesus promised that same power to the church before He ascended into heaven:

But ye shall receive power, after that the Holy Ghost is come upon you: and ye shall be witnesses unto me both in

Jerusalem, and in all Judaea, and in Samaria, and unto the uttermost part of the earth (Acts 1:8).

This is *dunamis* power, the ability, might, and strength to do the supernatural. It is this miracle-working power that heals and delivers. It is this power that will keep and preserve you. This same power will correct you and bring conviction when you go wrong. It is this power that saves people when you preach.

The promised power was released in prayer and the church stayed empowered through prayer. The church that is sharing the life-changing power of the Gospel is the church that is committed to prayer. The church that prevails over pressures and attacks from within and without is the church that prays without ceasing.

In Acts 12 we saw how the apostle James was killed by King Herod, and now Peter was arrested. It seemed a hopeless, destructive cycle of just holding on while going through fire. With one trial after the other, the persecution was only getting more intense, and change seemed impossible. Yet the church held on and stuck with what they knew. They prayed.

Things came to a head for Peter as we see in Acts 12:4:

And when they had seized him and put him in prison, delivering him over to four squads of soldiers to guard him, intending after the Passover to bring him out to the people.

Peter was dragged into custody like a common criminal. In prison, he was under maximum security, bound and guarded by sixteen soldiers. He was totally under their control—or so it seemed—until prayer changed the equation. As the church prayed, they enforced God's will.

We, too, want to enforce God's will in our own circumstances as we see mounting pressure on the righteous. Jeremiah 29:11 says, *"For I know the thoughts that I think toward you, saith the Lord, thoughts of peace, and not of evil, to give you an expected end."* "Expected end" means God is saying, "I am going to give you a future. I am going to give you hope. I am going to give you something to look forward to."

> *What you are going through may be challenging, but prayer should remind you it is not over yet.*

The enemy may have his time in our lives, but he will never have control. Church, rise up and pray. Right now, we see increasing unrest in our society. There is shooting and killing in the streets, in the schools, and in the malls. There is road rage. There is violence. Young people are being shot and brought into gangs. There are wars and rumors of war. Prices are going out of control. Too many of our potentially productive men are in prison.

What you are going through may be difficult, but prayer should remind you it is not over yet. It is not hopeless. God assures us that all things will work for our good because we love Him and are chosen of Him. For those who have trusted God, there were times in your life when it looked like the enemy was about to win—and then God intervened. He will do it again.

Prayer Can Reverse Fortunes

In 2 Chronicles 20, Moab and Ammon united their forces against the nation of Judah under King Jehoshaphat. They are described as a great multitude, implying not just their size but their intensity and ferocity, causing turmoil among God's people.

The Bible says King Jehoshaphat was terrified. Now, he could have panicked and surrendered outright. Or he could have used reason and consulted with his military strategists on the best line of defense. He did neither. Instead, he waited on the Lord for direction and called the entire nation to prayer and fasting to seek the Lord.

Standing before the community, Jehoshaphat prayed, "*O LORD God of our fathers, art not thou God in heaven? and rulest not thou over all the kingdoms of the heathen? and in thine hand is there not power and might, so that none is able to withstand thee?*" (Verse 6) Recounting the Lord's mighty deeds in the past, he brought their plight before Him and asked for His help.

Suddenly, one of the Levites from among them was moved to prophesy. There was a word released from the Lord in prayer. As you read this passage, make a note of the number of times the word "listen," or words to that effect, are used:

> He said, "**Listen**, all you people of Judah and Jerusalem! **Listen**, King Jehoshaphat! This is what the LORD says: Do not be afraid! Don't be discouraged by this mighty army, for the battle is not yours, but God's. Tomorrow, march out against them. You will find them coming up through the ascent of Ziz at the end of the valley that opens into the wilderness of Jeruel. But you will not even need to fight. Take your positions; then stand still and watch the LORD's victory. He is with you, O people of Judah and Jerusalem. Do not be afraid or discouraged. Go out against them tomorrow, for the LORD is with you!"

> Early the next morning the army of Judah went out into the wilderness of Tekoa. On the way Jehoshaphat stopped and said, "**Listen** to me, all you people of Judah and Jerusalem! Believe in the LORD your God, and you will be able to stand firm. Believe in his prophets, and you will succeed." After consulting the people, the king appointed singers to walk ahead of the army, singing to the LORD and praising him for his holy splendor. This is what they sang:

> "Give thanks to the LORD; his faithful love endures forever!" (2 Chronicles 20:15-17; 20-21 NLT, emphasis added)

Why was a listening mode so crucial? Because the enemy was so menacing that if they listened to their heartbeat, they would have fainted. Because God's strategy was so radical that only those who really listened and were attentive would receive the courage to follow through.

What was the outcome of all that listening?

At the very moment they began to sing and give praise, the LORD caused the armies of Ammon, Moab, and Mount Seir to start fighting among themselves. The armies of Moab and Ammon turned against their allies from Mount Seir and killed every one of them. After they had destroyed the army of Seir, they began attacking each other. So when the army of Judah arrived at the lookout point in the wilderness, all they saw were dead bodies lying on the ground as far as they could see. Not a single one of the enemy had escaped (2 Chronicles 20:22-24 NLT).

The Bible says it took three days to collect all the plunder that the enemy had left behind. They prayed and the Lord sent the word that said, "The battle is not yours, but God's." It looks bad, sometimes, for so many of us, but our hope is in Jesus.

Keep on praying.

Keep on asking for help. Keep on seeking Him. Pour out your heart to Him. Call upon His name. Refocus your ear to what the Lord is saying. Remember, if you do not have the pastor's number or anyone to text, say to yourself, "The Lord is with me. I am not alone."

The Lord is my shepherd; I shall not want.

He maketh me to lie down in green pastures: he leadeth me beside the still waters.

He restoreth my soul: he leadeth me in the paths of righteousness for his name's sake.

Yea, though I walk through the valley of the shadow of death, I will fear no evil: for thou art with me ... (Psalm 23:1-4)

Yes, the Lord is with you in every circumstance. You are not alone and you are not without resources. You have a mouth. Remember that He inhabits the praises of His people (See Psalm 22:3). You also have a listening ear, and you can recognize God's voice when He speaks, and confidently respond to what He says.

The prayers of the saints in Acts 12 caused Peter to be released. As Peter was released, he was awakened by an angel, chains fell off, and gates opened. Peter knew the Lord had rescued him. The Lord pulled Peter out of a situation he could have never gotten out of himself. The church prayed and God moved!

Church, will you pray? Prayer still works. God still hears and answers prayer. Countless people are in bondage. However, the prayers of the church can and will cause many to be rescued. Church, pray!

End of Chapter Reflection

What scripture in this chapter resonated with you the most? Why?

_____

_____

_____

_____

_____

_____

List at least three key principles from this chapter.

1. _____

_____

2. _____

_____

3. _____

_____

How will your prayer life change based on the principles presented in this chapter?

_____

_____

_____

_____

_____

_____

Prayer Time: Write a prayer asking God to help you apply the principles you have learned from this chapter.

_____

_____

_____

_____

_____

_____

_____

_____

CONCLUSION

Given the events occurring in the world today, there is a mandate for the church to pray. Violence covers the land. Mass shootings are happening almost every day. We aren't safe in our homes, schools, stores, malls, hospitals, and even in our churches. This is not the time for us to run and hide, to stay in our homes, or to live in fear. 2 Timothy 1:7 lets us know, *"For God hath not given us the spirit of fear; but of power, and of love, and of a sound mind."* We have power and this power is wrought through prayer.

In this book, we have discussed how we should take time to listen for God to speak when we are praying, and then we are to obey what God says. We are to pray persistently, pray without ceasing, and pray in our secret place. We must walk in authority and power.

When Peter was thrown into prison, the church prayed all night long. God answered their prayers, and Peter was miraculously released from prison.

Through all that is happening in our lives and in our churches, we must keep our focus. When our prayers are not being answered the way we think they should, if the answer is taking a long time to be manifested, or when we are bombarded with bad news, we must focus our thoughts on what Jesus said, "Fear not. Only believe."

Sometimes when we pray, things happen in life that cause us to lose our focus. It is during those difficult, trying times that we have to refocus our ears. We have to shut out the taunts of the enemy. When Jehoshaphat was faced with an impossible situation, he prayed and had to refocus his ears on the word God sent through Jahaziel: The battle is the Lord's!

God has given us authority and power. Let us walk in that authority. Let us use the power God has given us. Church, pray!

ABOUT THE AUTHOR

Bishop Arthur F. Mosley is one of the most dynamic speakers, educators, and authors of the 21st century. Widely respected by communities and leaders around the world, Bishop Mosley delivers a message of hope, inspiration, and unity. As an adolescent, he offered his gift of musicianship as an organist to the church. After serving in the Marines, Bishop Mosley attended California State University, where he earned a Bachelor's Degree in Liberal Studies. Additionally, Bishop Mosley attended C. H. Mason Theological Seminary, where he earned a Master of Divinity Degree, and later earned a Doctor of Ministry Degree from Knox Theological Seminary. Bishop Mosley's ministry was cultivated as he served and gleaned from the leadership of his uncle, Superintendent Arthur Clayton, II, his stepfather, Superintendent Monroe Magee, Dr. E. V. McGhee, and Bishop Joseph Hogan at New Life Tabernacle COGIC.

While attending New Life Tabernacle, he met and married the love of his life, Lady Shelia Mosley. Bishop and Lady Mosley's union was blessed with two daughters, Amber and Amanda. They were also blessed with one granddaughter, Maci Elaine Mosley, and their sons-in-love, Randall Richardson and Geoffery Foster. In 1992, Bishop Mosley answered his pastoral call and founded the Restoration Church of God in Christ in his home. Like his father, Pastor Freddie Mosley, Bishop Arthur Mosley also founded a second church, Family of God Church of God in Christ in 1994.

In 2002, Bishop Arthur F. Mosley became the pastor of the Cathedral of Faith COGIC, where he continues to serve as pastor. Bishop Mosley also currently serves as the Superintendent of the Light of the World District and as an administrative assistant in the North Central Georgia Jurisdiction. With a passion for spreading the Gospel across the world, Bishop Mosley has done mission work in Africa, Thailand, London, the Solomon Islands, Indonesia, Malaysia, and several other countries.

As a tenured educator, Bishop Mosley has served as Interim Dean of Education, Seminary Professor, and Professor of World Religions, Humanities, and College Success at Georgia Piedmont College. In 2021, Bishop Mosley was elevated in the Church of God in Christ to the office of Bishop of the Barbados First West Indies Ecclesiastical Jurisdiction. Bishop Mosley has remained a distinguished man of humility, kindness, and servitude, and his passion for souls and powerful ministry have made him a father, mentor, and inspiration to many.

To contact Bishop Mosley regarding speaking engagements, please use the information below.

Bishop Arthur F. Mosley
afmoslty@cofcogic.org
404-752-8960